Diary of a
PEARL HARBOR
Survivor

Alfred Benjamin Kameeiamoku Rodrigues

A Native Son's Memories of Pearl Harbor
and the War in the Pacific

PACIFIC
HISTORIC PARKS
★ Remember ★ Honor ★ Understand ★

ISBN: 978-1-936626-35-9

Table of Contents

Preface

At the urging of my eldest son, I went to visit the *Arizona* Memorial at Pearl Harbor in the spring of 2001. It had been a very long time since I had been there – and under very different circumstances. Of course, I had mixed emotions. But feeling the solemnity of the site and the reverence visitors gave it, I began to feel more at ease. So many visitors, of all ages and from all over the world, came to pay their respects to those who lost their lives on December 7, 1941. They also came to learn what it was like that day on December 7, 1941 – not so much out of curiosity but in an attempt to somehow share in that moment of history. Hence, I decided that I would indeed volunteer there – as my son said, it was my duty to do so.

Three times a week I once again put on a uniform – this time of the Pearl Harbor Survivor volunteers. There are still a few of us left, though the numbers keep dwindling as the days go by. We greet visitors, answer questions, take photos with them and sign the history books they buy at the bookstore. After my name, I always write the initials PHS. They assume it means Pearl Harbor Survivor. But I tell them it really stands for "Poor Hawaiian Sailor."

My eldest son once again urged me to step out of my comfort zone – this time he wanted me to publish the diary I kept of my days on the USS *Washington*, the battleship on which I served throughout the major battles of the Pacific after that day of infamy.

I could not disagree with his reasoning – people want to know what it was really like. Not just from an historian's perspective but from that of every-day people, like their fathers and grandfathers and uncles who did not get a chance to share their stories. And he was correct again -- it is my duty.

My Early Years

I was born on the island of Kauai, Territory of Hawaii on February 7, 1920. The family moved to Honolulu when I was about two where my mother, a school teacher, taught. We lived on Keeaumoku Street in Honolulu and took a street car home which passed a Dairyman's Ice Cream Parlor. Mom says I always wanted to get off there, which we did quite often to please my appetite. Thanks Mom.

The street car was the best way to get around in those days. We used to take a ride to Waikiki and crossed over a bridge in a swampy area into Waikiki. At that age there were no high rises and I don't remember many hotels, so I can say that all we could see was coconut trees and other foliage.

We returned to Kauai when my mother was offered a job to teach at the Kapaa School which was on a hill. We lived in a two-bedroom teachers cottage adjoining the school grounds and it was real easy for my Mom to go to work. Many days she would come home for lunch and make sandwiches for some of the children in her class who either forgot their lunches or who had eaten it before coming to school.

My mother died when I was eight years old and I felt like I wanted to die also. I loved her so much. They tell me that I cried every day for about two months after she left us and were very concerned about my health. They say time heals all wounds and it apparently does, but the memory stays with you forever.

Alfred (nickname "Sonny") with his father Alfred, mother Alice and younger sister Nani.

We then had to move to a plantation house in the town of Kealia right behind the store where my Dad worked as a salesman. We lived next to my Portuguese family and after a few months, I settled down and enjoyed the Portuguese bread one of my Aunts made in an outside oven. Mmmm, those were the days of good food.

My Dad was Portuguese and my Mom was part Hawaiian and part English. In those days it was not appropriate to marry outside of your race. Consequently, my Portuguese family looked down on my Dad and Mom.

From what I learned later, my mother realized this but being very patient, and the word is *hoomanawanui* in Hawaiian, she said it would go away soon. She invited some of the Portuguese families over for dinner and also had paid some of the teen-age girls to care for me when she had to do some work at school. One of those girls was Clementine Rapozo, and later married a Costa, who I loved so much as she cared for me while Mom was not at home. Many years later I lived with my sister when I first joined the Navy and Clementine, then married to Costa, lived only a block away. It was nice seeing her again. And Clementine retired as a school teacher.

Waianae sportsman Alfred Rodrigues poses proudly beside his homemade surfboard at Pokai Bay in 1932 while his fans look on. That's his sister, Nani, nearest his left.

Kauai is geologically the oldest island of the group of islands and, without any personal prejudice, the most beautiful of all. I have been to all of the islands and that is my opinion; and as politicians would say, I approve this message.

When my Dad retired from the plantation, it was another move again. We rented a house in Kapaa right next to a Chinese family named Shak. Mr. Shak was the Treasurer of the Pineapple Cannery we had in town and he was a golfer. He had three sons younger than myself and one day he asked me if I could caddie for him and I quickly said yes, but I had never done it before. He told me not to worry, it was easy.

In those days the bags were very light compared to what they have today. They played at the Waialua Golf Course which was only nine holes then and we got paid twenty five cents a round and usually got a ten cent tip. That was good money and there were times when no other caddy would show up and I would carry two bags so I made seventy cents. Two bags, however, were not that easy as you had to run around for two players, but the pay was nice.

On Saturdays Mr. Shak did not play so I walked or hitched a ride to the course, found a bag and caddied eighteen holes. It was only a nine hole course but they played it twice from different teeing areas.

I went to Kauai High School in the town of Lihue about ten miles from home. There was always someone with a car with whom we shared the gas. There was no other transportation then. We got to know students from every town in Kauai until the Waimea High School was built a year or so later.

I played football, volleyball, basket ball and baseball and was also on the swimming team so kept busy. The only wrong thing I did was to take up smoking, so there went my caddy money. I finally quit smoking when I retired from the Navy.

After high school I decided to go live with my sister Nani who had moved to Honolulu and was working for a family by the name of Reese. He was Norwegian and was the treasurer for the Hawaiian Telephone Company. He had three sons and they had a smaller house on the lot where I stayed and enjoyed it very much.

The Reese family had a country home in Punaluu and the Dad always had friends down for the weekend and had big parties, barbecuing and lots of booze. Dad always had a case in one of the bathrooms, where all the kids could find it, so we also had our own parties.

Their house was right next to David Kaapu a Hawaiian family who actually lived in a grass hut and it was a tourist attraction. One year Shirley Temple visited the place and we could look over the fence to see her. That was when she used to sing "The Good Ship Lollypop"; no young person knows that song, of course. Anyway it was fun to stay with the Reese family.

One night I met my cousin Arthur who was going to join the Naval Reserves and he invited me to one of their meetings. Being only seventeen years old we needed our parents permission to enlist. I sent the application to my Dad on Kauai and he approved, while Arthur's Dad did not.

In the Navy

Each year in the Naval Reserves, we were assigned to some ship for a two-week training period. One year it was a seagoing tug the *Whippoorwill*, and we went to the Palmyra Atoll. We waded in waters with baby sharks and saw giant crabs open coconuts with their claws. Another year we were assigned to the USS *Tracy*, a four-stacker destroyer, and that is where I decided to become a storekeeper.

When I first joined the Navy, my ambition was to be an engineer. On the *Tracy* my first duty was in the fire room. The first day on board they gave me a two-hour watch and it sure was hot. While I was having my dinner that evening, one of the petty officers yelled at me and said I was supposed to be in the engine room to relieve the watch there. I went down to the fire room and ten minutes later I passed out from the heat. They carried me out and I never went back again.

In the morning, George Maile, the Chief Storekeeper who happened to be a neighbor of mine, asked me if I wanted to be a storekeeper. I jumped at the chance. It made a difference on the rest of my career in the Navy.

Prior to the war, there was a Chief Storekeeper Slogeris who played golf, along with myself and two other storekeepers, three times a week -- on Wednesdays (which was called a Rope Yarn Sunday or a half day of work), again on Saturday afternoon and then on Sunday. We all shot in the mid seventies and always had dinner at the Kemoo Farms Restaurant which was right outside the main gate at Schofield Barracks. A sizzling steak was less than two dollars which included all the trimmings plus your choice of beverages. A mug of beer was no more than twenty cents. The name of the course was the Kalakaua Golf Course which was a par 72. It no longer is there today. It is covered with military housing. How sad.

In November, about one hundred twenty of the local reserves were called to active duty and we reported to the Receiving Station, Pearl Harbor. It was near the main gate. At that time I owned a motorcycle but they were restricted from entering Pearl Harbor. So I parked it outside the fence next to the Bloch Arena. I could see it from the second deck of our living quarters and always saw sailors sitting on it and it worried me, so I decided to sell it.

One remembrance of the motorcycle was having Steamboat Mokuahi, a nice big Hawaiian friend of mine and also in the Naval Reserves, ride with me to the Naval Base every morning. We sure were a sight to see. His son Sam was a famous surfer on Waikiki beach.

About a month before December 1941, we started holding air raid drills. It was an omen that something was to happen.

Alfred (Navy nickname "Rod", left) with
fellow Navy mates and golfing buddies
John Mino (center) and Varney Moore (left).

Day of Infamy

On December 7, 1941, I had the four-to-eight watch; and the officer of the deck, who was a quartermaster second class, told me that they had received a message at 3:30 AM that our destroyer the USS *Ward* had dropped depth charges on an unidentified submarine and sunk it.

At 7:45 AM, I went to have breakfast and had just put my tray down when we could hear explosions from the shipyard area. We assumed that they were doing some dredging work and thought nothing about it until the General Alarm sounded.

We all ran out to the armory where they issued us .30 caliber rifles or .45 pistols. We then saw the planes overhead with the red insignia on the bottom of their wings and we knew they were Japanese planes.

They were flying low enough that you could see the pilots faces. We heard yells to shoot the pilot as they had open cockpits. Hell, it was hard enough to shoot the airplane much less the pilot. With a rifle of 1941 vintage, you could only shoot one bullet at a time then cock the rifle before shooting the next shot, and by then the plane was out of reach.

The whole battle lasted a little over two hours and all of the eight battleships in the harbor were damaged or sunk plus dozens of other ships and over two thousand deaths including 1,177 on the USS *Arizona* itself.

When the Officers came aboard after the call for all military personnel to report to their duty stations, one of the officers took my rifle away and ordered me to open the warehouse to issue supplies.

That evening some of our planes from the carrier USS *Enterprise* were returning to Ford Island to land. Some itchy fingered sailor started shooting at them and you could see the sky light up with red flares. One or two were shot down and the rest went to other airfields on the island to land safely.

Another incident happened after the second wave of planes left. A Japanese farmer who collected slop cans for his pig farm was turned away by one of the Chiefs who pointed his rifle and told him to leave or get shot. We had to calm the Chief as it was obvious that he meant it.

We were restricted from using the telephones so there was no way for me to let my sister know that I was well. The next morning a friend who was delivering bread to our post came on board, and I asked him to inform her that her brother was alive and well. It was a relief to do that.

In the mean time, we were adding more bunks to make room for sailors from ships who lost everything. Our population of the base just about doubled and it was a completely different environment having sailors from many states in the Union amongst us.

On or about the later part of February, I got orders to go to the island of Kauai where they were setting up a receiving station like the one we were at. Their mission was to provide logistics to small craft, mostly sampans formerly used by local fishermen as their means of living. These sampans were confiscated by the military for their use to patrol the waters around the islands watching for enemy ships or subs.

Being back on the island I was born on was quite a thrill, especially since many of the islanders had never seen sailors before. We had a Lieutenant (two bars, which equates to a Captain in the Army or Marines) and most of the population called him Captain and he never did reveal his real grade.

At that time storekeepers also did the payroll so I spent a lot of time at a desk making sure everybody got their pay which was not much in those days.

In May, they sent me back to Pearl Harbor and it was nice to go back home. Kauai is country and a nice place to live; but after a few years in a bigger city, it does get boring, especially at nights where there was not much entertainment.

At one of my visits to the Naval Supply Center to submit some requisitions for supplies for our storeroom, I met another storekeeper from the USS *Washington* (BB56) and we started chatting. He told me all about his ship and it was very interesting. He was leaving the ship shortly and going to new construction back in the states. Being curious and wanting to leave the islands, I asked him if there was a possibility for me to get aboard. We met two days later and arranged for my transfer. It was easier than expected.

Let me confess that the prime reason I wanted a transfer was to get far away from the Islands because of a very nice lady I was intimate with when I was on the island of Kauai. She kept hinting of marriage and I certainly was not ready to raise a bunch of curtain climbers and rug rats.

BB56, USS Washington

On June 21, 1943, I reported aboard the mighty battleship USS *Washington* which happened to be in a dry dock that day. Storekeeper First Class C.B. Wilson greeted me in the Supply Office and took me around to introduce me to all of the supply personnel.

We left dry dock on the 22nd and tied up to pier B-16 and I did the chores assigned to a storekeeper. At that time I was a First Class Storekeeper. There were 21 supply personnel in a compartment the size of a normal bedroom in your home. Talk about toe jams and other smells. Unfortunately, I had the fifth bunk on top and had to be careful getting in and out of the bunk.

On the 27th I was invited to a luau and asked Wilson to go along. Since overnight liberty was not granted to anyone, Wilson said not to worry he would take care of it. So we both took a large garbage can like we were going to the trash bin on the pier and hid it behind the bin. When we returned in the morning we took the trash cans aboard ship and no one was the wiser. Of course, there were two gang planks, so we used the one that was manned by a petty officer and not an Officer. Wilson introduced me to other tricks of the trade.

On the 29th we left Pearl for gunnery practice and passed Maui, then around the big island of Hawaii, and then returned to Pearl Harbor on the 4th of July.

My War Diary

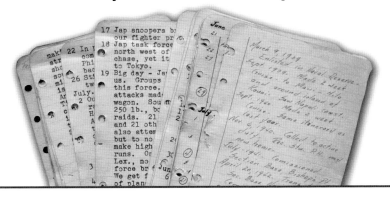

rom my time on the USS *Washington* to the day of my transfer to a new assignment I kept a diary and the following is what I recorded…

June 21, 1943
Wilson, C.B. SK 1C shows me around the ship. Whatta ship.

June 22
Left dry-dock – tied to Pier B-16.

June 27
Went to luau. Took Wilson, got soused. Met Ida Gulick. Got back to ship at 2300 – over leave. Sneaked aboard all right.

June 29
Left for Gunnorf

July 1
Not standing watches as yet. This duty ain't so bad. Saw the Island of Hawaii – so near yet so far.

July 4
Return to Pearl.

July 8
Boil on right arm – bad blood.

July 19
Liberty. Stayed at Gregg's overnight.

July 21
Leave Pearl. Dope is we will be back shortly.

July 24
Return to Pearl.

July 27
Liberty cancelled – what luck. Seems like I won't see Sis for some time to come. Leave Pearl at 1730 -- destination unknown. Dope is we go to Noumea.

July 28
Course due south. Two transports said to be the Lurline *and* Mt. Vernon *plus a number of Tin Cans. Played poker. Made forty dollars.*

July 29
Me a pollywog - huh - Got a hair cut and it did not cost a penny. Baldy they call me now.

July 30
Got a subpoena. Crossed the line at 1300. ("Subpoena" is part of the ceremony and it was all in fun. Some of the sailors get out of hand and occasionally a few will land in the sick bay for cuts and bruises.)

July 31
Landed in the sick bay. Infection on right arm. Missed ceremony. Ha! Ha!

August 1
Still in sick bay. Get out tomorrow.

August 3
Tuesday or I should say Wednesday. We crossed International date line. Getting cold.

August 7
GQ. Going in port. Havannah Harbor, Island of Efati, New Hebrides group. Swish – anchor brake doesn't work. 12 tons go overboard including chain and 3 men. No one hurt. (The 3 men were from the supply division. This happened on the port side where the supply department holds muster daily. Fortunately no one was hurt -- only three men went swimming without permission. Divers from one of the Repair ships retrieved the anchor the next day.)

August 8
Mailed a few letters. Nothing doing.

August 9
Only reason for going on the beach is to have a couple of beers.

August 26
Mail from Sis – 2 letters.

August 30
All ships leave Havannah Harbor.

September 3
Position 8" Lat, 165" Long. Nearest Japanese base 360 miles. Guadalcanal a few miles away.

September 5
Going back to Efati today noon.

September 8
North Carolina *leaves. Dope is she is going back to Bremerton via Pearl.*

September 22
Underway at 0730. Massachusetts *goes with us.*

September 23
Return to Efati.

September 26
Go to church -- try not to miss Mass.

September 29
Received mail from [Varney] Moore (the golfing buddy in Hawaii).
He wants me to join him for some kind of business enterprise after this
war. I think I will.

October 5.
Payday. Sent Nani (sister) thirty pounds for birthday present. Received
first Honolulu Star Bulletin dated August 21st. Dull life. (Most of the
news, regardless of where the paper was printed, did not give much
details of what we were doing in the Pacific. We heard more propa-
ganda over the radio from English speaking Japanese stations and it
was good for laughs.)

October 7
All ships leave harbor for tactical exercise.

October 10
Return to Efati after three strenuous days of maneuvers. There were 17
GQs. Just as soon go into actual battle, or stay in port.

October 11
0645. Here we go again. Leave port with destroyer escorts. 1525, boy
that was a close shave, a torpedo crosses our bow. Result, returning
to port at full speed.

October 29
Got stuck with S.P. duty. Got drunk, but returned to ship alright.

October 30
All ships leave Efati. Our boats are on board indicating that we may not come back again to this port.

November 2
Rendezvous at sea. Meet 4 Battlewagons, 3 Carriers. Ships are Indiana, Tennessee, Maryland *and* Colorado. *Carriers are* Bunker Hill, Essex, Independence. *Dope sheet shells out with straight info. We will be in Nandi Waters, Fiji's by the 7th.*

November 5
Money order $50 to Sis. Mele Kalikimaka.

November 7
Fiji in sight. Moored at 1007 Nandi Waters.

November 8
Saw first woman since we left Pearl. Bought pictures for album. Boy does a white woman look good. But no touchee. (While in Fiji a few of the crew bought shrunken heads, ugh! When the commanding officer heard about it, they were all confiscated and no one knows what they did with them.)

November 11
Here we go again. 1000, all ships leave Nandi. Scuttlebutt says we may see action in five or six moons, perhaps sooner.

November 11
150 miles NW of Fiji. DC puts out straight slugs. We will see action before we go in again. Two weeks will be least number of days out this trip. Then we may not put in till next year. Hope this will be a decisive battle so we may all go home.

November 12
Friday, still the 12th. Crossed date line. Position Lat. 80° S., 176° W. Long. Dope is we will bombard Nauru.

November 13
Getting hotter as we near the equator. 4° S. Lat, 176° W long

November 14
Crossed equator – won't be long before the battle begins.

November 15
Met North Carolina *and 6 Carriers. There are 6 wagons now and about a dozen cans. Tanker comes alongside. We fuel and receive some mail. None for me. Hot scoop -- 3 wagons and 3 flat tops will act as interceptors while troops land on Gilberts. Main objective is to draw out Jap fleet. If so, we have task forces near enough to take on any size Jap fleet. Carriers with us are the* Lexington, Yorktown *and* Cowpence.

November 16
Still fueling ships. Saw "Buck Private" [the movie] again with Abbott and Costello – or vice versa. May see action – everything tense.

November 17
Our advance forces attack Makin, Gilbert and Marshals at 0600. This morning we were 600 miles away from both islands. We go on condition 2 tomorrow. (Condition 2 is set when an impending action is expected.)

November 18
Gilbert and Marshals attacked again by our advanced forces. 300 miles away from islands. Will be 100 away by morning. The heat is terrific -- 83° temp early in the mornings. Nauru also attacked. We will aid in landing troops.

November 19
Planes from our force attacks. Tarawa, Mili and Makin are under constant bombing by our planes.

November 20
We attack again. Troops are landing. Not much opposition. We have not fired yet. We fuel the Nicholas *(449) and (582) [destroyer].*

November 21
GQ 0235, Jap planes out on the hunt. Radar picks up 12 planes.
Come within 8 miles, darkness protects us.

November 22
G.Q. General Alarm, 0800, bogey turns out to be friendly. Fueled tin
cans at 1730, we expect to bombard Mili tomorrow.

November 23
0530 -- Our troops have captured Makin. 60 percent of the troops
have landed. Got [radio station] KGU this morning while on G.Q.,
homesick that's all, at 063 it was 0800 Pearl time. May bombard
later on during the day. G.Q., General Alarm at 1000, 18 Jap planes
try to attack our task force. Our fighters bag12, 3 more aflame and
the rest were base bound. We are between Makin and Mili. Had
another G.Q. at 2000, bogeys are friendly. Troops take Tarawa.

November 24
G.Q. at 1225. Jap planes try to go in, our fighters down and disperse
group. 36 planes shot.

November 25
Usual Thanksgiving dinner. Left immediate battle area to fuel.
Received mail from tanker, 1 letter from Sis. No dope on movements.

November 26
Nothing much doing. Saratoga *with us. Other carriers joined new*
task group. 1754, I take it back, General Alarm. Jap snoopers attack
North Carolina, *task force.*

November 27
1234 General Alarm, Jap snipers around us. 1805 -- we fire our port
5" Guns. Planes come within 2000 yards. No results as yet. Heard
"Pistol Packing Mama" for the first time.

November 28
Here they come again. 1820 G.Q., we bag two, probably three. Fired more tonight than last night.

November 29
No attacks. Shucks.

November 30
Fuel cans (589). Nothing doing. Holy Xmas, there just went a few explosions. Cans dropping cans. Sub contact. Hope they get them.

December 1
Well here it is December 1. Wonder how long we'll be out? Fueled ships today. Sent mail. My Xmas cards are on their way, I hope. Sub contact. Our cans drop 60 to 70 charges. From three to four subs in vicinity. No results.

December 2
Our force of scouts bag 1 Betty. Getting tired. These Condition 2 watches sure come fast.

December 3
Nothing new. Tarawa attacked by big force of Jap planes. We go on G.Q., sub contact. No results.

December 4
Be Xmas soon. Must have lots of mail for me some place. We must provision ship soon. Hope we go to Pearl.

December 5
Saw one of our planes shoot a Betty. Nice sight. (This was the first time I got stuck topside when G.Q. sounded. Could not get below as every hatch was closed and could not be opened from the main deck. It sure was scary.)

December 6
Fueled ship again. New dope is that we bombard Nauru. We crossed the line again. 5° South of equator.

December 7
Here it is, Dec. 7 again -- Two long years since the war began. Lots of things have happened since. Oh well, big day tomorrow. 6 BB's will open fire on Nauru. Will start with 9 gun salvo simultaneously from each ship, then go on for half hour or so. BB's are North Carolina, South Dakota, Massachusetts, Alabama, Indiana *and the mighty* Washington, *that's us. Hope we make out all right. Also, 8 cans to screen us if necessary.*

December 8
We bombard Nauru. First salvo at 0704. 135 16" shells and 400 5" shells from each ship. Can loses 27 men from Jap 5" (getting too close to the shore) in attempt to save two pilots. AA strong at beginning but went out almost completely. Island covered with smoke as we leave. Also planes attack from carriers. We are heading back to Port.

December 10
We finally move ahead one day. We should have moved ahead days ago when we crossed the date line, but there must have been a reason for not doing so. Boyd (544) *comes alongside [for fueling]. She was the can that lost some men. Of the 27 casualties, 10 died. Looked all beat up. (We passed many gallons of ice cream by high line and they were real happy.)*

December 11
Will be in tomorrow. Got S.P. duty, soon as we arrive in port. Oh well.

December 12
After 31 days at sea we finally settle down again. Mail coming aboard and then some.

December 13
S.P. duty. Letters, letters, letters.

December 16
Letter from Jenel Moore. Nothing new, working like hell.

December 25
Xmas. Went to midnight Mass last night. Well, no rest for the weary.
We leave Havannah at 1030. North Carolina *tags along plus 4 cans.*

December 26
We plan to intercept a small Jap task force that is trying to re-enforce bases in Bougainville and Rabaul.

December 27
A couple of hundred miles from Henderson field.

December 31
New Years Eve. No action. Temp 84 yesterday, 79 this morning.

1944

January 1
Ho hum, what a life. Another year, another hundred thousand dollars. Like heck.

January 2
Going back to Efati.

January 3
Wrong. Turned around last night. Going north again.

January 4
Above Rabaul. Position Lat 3" S., Long 155" W. Bad place to be. No ships in sight. Our carrier force may have done the job for us.

January 5
Going home to Efati. Hope we make it. Want some mail.

January 8
Return to base. Moor at 1000.

January 9
Provision ship. GSK Stores from Antares.

January 10
Provision ship again from Aldeberan.

January 18
Shoving off again. All ships leave harbor.

January 19
Funa Futi in the Ellice island is our destination.

January 20
Crossed date line. Thursday comes twice. Sure is a big lagoon, but you can see right across the island. We sure get a lot of ships in the harbor now. 56 in all including merchants and tankers.

January 22
The New Jersey *and* Iowa *come in. What ships. That makes 8 wagons out here now.*

January 23
Bye bye Funa Futi, hope we never do see you again. This looks like the big push they have been waiting for. Marshall Islands here we come.

January 27
Crossed equator at 0800 this morning. Our forces have been divided. This task force consists of the Massachusetts, Indiana, Yorktown, Lexington, *3 cruisers and about 18 cans. We will shell Kwajalein Sunday or Monday.*

January 28
Fueled cans 667, 668, 669, 670 and 629.

January 29
We lay out while planes bomb Malaloit. Tomorrow we shell.

January 30
1000 - First salvo on chain of islands of the Kwajalein group. We make quite a mess. Last salvo fires at 1430. Expended 350 16" shells and 2179 5" shells. Wonder when the folks back home will hear about this. Squadron of B-24's fly over towards us, low on the horizon. No recognition signals given. Tin can and carrier open up on them. Shoot one down. Too bad. Can picks up all but one man. We lost three planes in the scrap this morning.

January 31
Fooling around.

February 1
Collision. We run smack into Indiana. *She crossed our bow when breaking formation to fuel cans. She takes full responsibility. It's the first time that I have been so scared since Pearl Harbor. Lose 60 feet of our focsle (the forward part of a ship). We will with no doubt at all go to some Navy Yard. We are cruising at 6 knots and will head for Mili [the Majuro Atoll]. 5 officers and 1 enlisted man die from results of collision. May see Pearl before long. Burial at sea of those who died. (Because it was so hot in our sleeping quarters, I decided to set up a cot in the supply office where it was somewhat cooler and the collision knocked me of the cot. We lost 90 feet of our bow.)*

February 2
Will make the Majuro atoll tonight to patch up a little then on to the navy yard.

February 3
Tie alongside the repair ship Vestal. Jack Courtney another local boy from Hawaii is on board.

February 7
24 years ago I made my debut into this land of the free, despite of what we pay for it.

February 11
1030 - Pearl, here we come. All the while in Majuro, we issued almost all of our stock to tin cans. There were more than a hundred ships in that lagoon. Nimitz and other men from DC come to see damage done.

February 18
1530 - Entering Pearl. G.Q. Well here we are again.

February 22
Go on five day leave. Will try to see Dad.

February 27
Could not make it home. Stayed with Nani (Sis) all the time.

March 2
Nani has baby boy.

March 6
Leaving Pearl today, 1120. Underway -- was not able to see baby. We probably will drop in at Pearl on our return out to southpac.

March 8
Getting cold as hell, literally speaking. Helped commissary steward in the cold storage, just to get used to it. (This was to get adjusted for our next stop in what we, in Hawaii, call the Mainland.)

March 10
Temperature 49 degrees. Will get in Sunday sometime, in Bremerton navy yard.

March 12
Dock – Puget Sound. It sure is cold out here. Liberty tonight, Whoopee.

April 19
Having good time. Go on ten day leave.
(Booze is not easy to acquire in Seattle. You need a ration card from the state and all the booze hounds applied for one. However, any cab driver can get you a bottle for a sum. One driver told me that since the Washington *arrived the price went up 5 dollars a bottle. What a rip off!)*

April 30
Darn it but time sure goes by fast. Had a very good time in the states and sure hate to leave. Leave Anchorage at 0600 and anchor at Port Angeles tonight sometime. Bye bye Seattle. Take on 500 passengers for Pearl.
(A group of sailors were making the rounds in Seattle and ended up in a night club where they played Benny Goodman music from a juke box and every body was having a good time and dancing A waitress named Dottie served us and just before closing I ordered a drink, handed Dottie a hundred dollar bill and told her to keep the change. I must have been drunk. Two nights later I visited the same night club and when Dottie spotted me she came over and said, "You forgot your change." I could not believe it and she insisted that I take it. I did and made a date for dinner the next evening which eventually made me spend the ten days leave. Got an apartment and Dottie was my guide the whole time I stayed in Seattle.)

May 2
We are heading for San Francisco. Dope says we will stay there for a day or two.

May 3
Golden Gate. Just like the pictures portray it. Passed Alcatraz, looks nice from the outside. Anchor a little ways from the Oakland Bay Bridge

May 5
Here we go again. Leave Frisco at 1200. Made two liberties there. Not bad. All women. Pearl bound.

May 10
Arrive in Pearl. See my new nephew. Cute, everybody fine. Tried to go home to Kauai [to see my Dad] but did not make it again.

May 14
Leave Pearl for gunnery [practice].

May 18
Return to Pearl.

May 24
Take on passengers. Leaving for that good old southpac. Did I say that? So long people.

May 29
Crossed date line. Lost Sunday. Will arrive in Majuro tomorrow.

May 30
Received 5 letters from Dottie. Dropped anchor at 1200.

June 6
All ships leave Majuro. Big doings pretty soon.

June 7
Good news at sea, about the invasion of Europe.

June 8
We will bombard the island of Saipan on the 13th. Our troops will invade on the 15th. Guam and the other islands will also be taken by the largest fleet ever assembled in the Pacific theater. May meet the Jap fleet. Everyone hopes so anyway for it shorten the war, we hope.

June 10
Jap snooper brought down by one of our carrier planes. Radar picked snooper at 23 miles southwest.

June 11
One more Jap plane downed. A Helen.

June 13
We bombard the island of Saipan. GQ at 1015. Secure at 1700. Firing all the time. After securing, we watch other ships fire on the island. All installations and most of their gun emplacements are destroyed or so we assume. It is a beautiful sight to see the other ships fire 16" salvos.

June 14
Taking it easy. Old battle wagons go in to finish up. Troops will invade tomorrow. Carrier force planes sink 10 Jap ships and damage 10 more. That once consisted of a convoy, undoubtedly reinforcement for Saipan. Guam is also attacked by a cruiser force.

June 15
Our troops are landing. Have some opposition. At present, about 8 tanks going inland, 800 yards or so. Second wave can be seen leaving the transports at sea. More opposition, this ain't a pushover -- 1800 G.Q., general alarm, group of torpedo planes attack our force. Every ship opens fire. This task force bags 14 planes and 1 probably. The planes come in at about 250 miles per hour. 1 plane drops its fish a few feet from our fantail with Lex as its objective. All ships fire at same plane. It starts burning so the pilot in a last stand apparently decides to make a suicidal crash dive on the carrier. Yet only a few yards from the Lexington, it starts climbing, missing the flight deck within a few yards, climbs to about 500 feet, then bursts into flames and glides toward the sea causing an enormous ball of fire on the surface of the water. Our cross fire strafes the can Carpenter, killing one man and injuring six, an inevitable accident.

June 16
No attacks - Fuel ships. Mail on some other tanker. At night, flashes, flares and gun shot can be seen and heard from the direction of Saipan, indicating a stiff resistance.

June 17
Jap snoopers brought down by our fighter protection.

June 18
Jap task force - 450 miles northwest of us. We may chase, yet it may be
too close to Tokyo.

June 19
Big day - Japs are out to get us. Groups of planes attack this force.
Dive bomber attacks made on every battle wagon. South Dakota *takes*
a 250 lb. bomb on one of these raids. 21 men die as results and 21
others injured. Planes also attempt some torpedo runs but to no
success. They also make high altitude bombing runs. One near miss
on the Lexington, *no damage. This task force brings down 15 planes.*
We get final reports on amount of planes brought down by our carrier
force planes. 358 sures, 28 probables, for the greatest air victory yet
in the war.

June 20
Our planes attach Jap task forces. Damage carriers and heavy craft,
possibly a wagon. Tomorrow morning another attack will be made.
We may catch up with Jap fleet yet. May turn back though, as we are
nearing the Philippines as will be subject to air attacks by land planes.

June 22
In pursuit of Jap fleet we come within 540 miles of the Philippines.
We are heading back towards Saipan.

June 26
Still at sea. Patrolling between and around the Marianas.

July 2
Our plane picks up pilot on raft about 100 yards off Guam.
He was on the raft for 17 days. At night he would paddle to the island
for coconuts, his only food then go out to sea during the day. We have
our first G.Q. since the 22nd. Nothing happens.

July 3
Almost one month at sea. Monotonous as hell.

July 4
To date on this cruise we have traveled 11,000 miles. Lots of miles, mostly circles thought.

July 7
At 0900 we drop anchor in an anchorage off Saipan. We see the destruction caused by our guns the day of bombardment. To the north of the island our troops are still driving the Japs toward the beach, while at sea our cruisers and cans keep constant fire on the enemy. All of this is plainly visible from our anchorage. Planes keep circling the battle area and frequently making what appears to be strafing runs. This is some show and all for free. To our south and not more than 6 or 7 miles away the Jap occupied island of Tinian can be seen. An estimated 7,000 troops occupy Tinian as we send planes and cans to ease an eventual landing by bombing with a little target practice for the boys. Sunk Jap freighters lie dead ahead. The same ships we hit on our first mission. The purpose of this anchorage was a conference with all combat Pac heads. We leave Saipan at 1700. While at anchor we provision supply and fuel tin cans that tie alongside port and starboard.

July 9
All resistance ceases in Saipan. Mopping up of snipers and recon-struction is underway.

July 13
We anchor off Saipan. Dead Jap bodies can be seen floating out to sea with the current. All are Japs that were driven towards the ocean and took the easy way out (by committing hara kiri).

July 15
At sea 40 days and only got mail once. May get mail on Tuesday when the Alabama *returns from Eniwetok.*

July 18
Finally get mail. 32 letters all told. 20 from Dottie. Not bad eh what!

July 20
Still at sea. Since the day we left port we have traveled 20,000 miles. Today our planes will bomb Palau. We are 60 miles north of the island.

August 12
Drop anchor in Eniwetok after traveling 26,000 miles. Lots of hard work ahead. Taking on supplies, ammunition and provisions and perhaps a few cases of beer. Eniwetok is like all atolls. The chiefs have a beer party on an island of their own. Okay, okay.

(Talking about chiefs, I should say that with all the GQ's, condition 2 watches and the regular supply work in between, I forgot to mention that I was promoted to SKC or a Storekeeper Chief. The chiefs' quarters aboard the Washington *was like moving from a shack to a mansion. We had our own mess boys, our own cook, you ordered what you wanted for breakfast -- what more could one ask for. Wide bunks and only two high. Thank you God.)*

August 30
After working a lot and going on 3 beer parties, we are pulling out to sea again. The Palau and Yap islands are our next objective. Scuttlebutt.

September 5
Still roaming out here. New Jersey *returns from Pearl. Halsey aboard her, but we still carry the combat Pac flag.*

September 12
After holding tactical exercises we join forces with the carrier task groups. We see the Philippines, the first time anyone has seen it since the war started. It seems the army has been bombing Mindanao with no air resistance and that is probably why we are so close to land. Air attacks from our carriers continue relentlessly through the day. Expect to be attacked by land based planes tonight. It was good to see land, however, with mountains on it [after all those atolls].

September 20
Today at noon we are again within striking distance of Leyte. After leaving this area to fuel and be near the landing forces on Palau. Air strikes are being staged today. We are 440 miles from Manila. If not detected before sunset, we will steam at full speed towards the island of Luzon and launch an air attack in the morning. Radio silence and our radars are cut out 'til morn.

September 21
Heavy rains in the morning but we launch attacks anyway. We are within 50 miles of the island of Luzon. In the evening we see Luzon only 30 miles distant. No attacks made on this task force yet, which consists of 16 carriers, 6 wagons and countless numbers of cruisers and tin cans.

September 27
Going back to Saipan.

September 28
Anchor in Saipan. Receive mail. No supply ships.

September 29
Leave Saipan, go to Ulithi atoll.

October 1
Anchor in Ulithi – it's just another atoll. You can't tell one from another. Reach Ulithi. Drop Anchor, provision ship.

October 3
Leave Ulithi. Storm coming up. It's nice and rough. May get seasick.

October 5
Return to Ulithi, still windy.

October 6
All ships leave Ulithi. A new carrier - John Hancock *- joins our forces.*
South Dakota *is also with us again.*
(We nicknamed the ship "The Shitty Dick", and you can imagine the
fights we have every time we meet them on beer parties, especially
when we use their nicknames. What's a black eye now and then.
Just good fun, then we have another beer.)

October 7
Waters still rough. It is said that we are on the edge of a typhoon. It is
wonderful to sight to watch the water break over our bow, completely
covering the focsle (the forward part of the ship). This trip will be a
long one according to bum dope. Possibly an air strike on Japan itself.

October 10
Weather changing. It was 86 degrees two days ago, 79 this morning.
The reason is that we have gone 800 miles north and today are 100
miles from Okinawa Shima -- a Jap base. Our planes attack and the
hunting seems plentiful. No straight dope yet. We are 400 miles or
less from Formosa.

October 11
Last night we left the immediate battle area to fuel. We are fueling
from a tanker today. Much damage was done yesterday. After fueling
we head for the direction of Formosa where we will conduct strikes
by carrier based planes. One man was electrocuted.

October 12
We are some 60 miles from Formosa and 230 miles from the China
coast. Burial at sea today [for the man who was electrocuted
yesterday].

October 13
After the attacks yesterday we went to G.Q. stations only to stay there
all night. All ships kept firing sporadically for most of the night. This
force gets 14 planes.

October 14
G.Q. at 1500 - Planes attack this force. More firing. Last night we got 7 planes. G.Q. lasted till 2200. The cruiser Canberra takes an aerial torpedo. Burial at sea for a man who was hit by shrapnel on tin can. Four other men from same tin can aboard here for treatment.

October 15
G.Q. general alarm at 1800. We are credited for two planes. They come within 200 yards of our starboard beam. Our 40 mm's get them. All night G.Q. off and on.

October 16
Our planes act as fighter protection for B-29's that bomb Formosa.

October 17
We leave this area and are proceeding to a fuel rendezvous whence we will go to the Philippines to assist in the invasion which is set for the 20th. No mail from Maxine or Nani. Leyte is the island that our troops will make landings on.

October 20
Mac Arthur's troops invade Leyte. Our forces support the landing. 600 transports carry the troops.

October 22
After starting back to Ulithi we are ordered to return to the battle area.

October 23
G.Q. all night. Japs send their fleet in to repulse landings. Three different forces approach the Philippines We go in to attack the force that is reported in the San Bernardino Strait, but another Jap force approaching from the north of Luzon alters our original plans, so we proceed north to meet this force.

October 24
We are now within striking distance of the force. Our planes make a strike and cripple them badly. We hope to meet them tonight. All night G.Q. We came within 90 miles of Jap fleet tonight but can't catch them. Our planes, however, sink 4 carriers plus other combat ships. It is said that our submarines may finish off the crippled ships. We have a ring of subs in this vicinity.

October 25
Jersey *and* Iowa *are dispatched to meet other Jap force in the Bernardino Straits. On the way down they encounter 1 Jap cruiser, sinking it. Our air force pounds third Jap task force and reports are vague as yet.*

October 26
Our carrier planes still pound Jap fleet. Latest reports claim 2 battleships definitely sunk, cruisers and cans also sunk, but correct figures are not yet verified.

October 27
We fuel from tanker. Our ships losses to date -- 1 carrier, 1 can sunk, 4 cruisers damaged. Honolulu *is one of the damaged cruisers. These reports have been confirmed though other ships may have suffered superficial damages.*

October 30
We are entering port. While here in Ulithi, we will provision ship then may go to Manus in the Admiralty's.

November 2
We leave Ulithi and are heading for Manus where they say are nice recreation facilities for the men. Incidentally, it has been five months since we have seen a woman – tch, tch!!!

November 3
Tough luck. Our course is now due west or towards the island of Leyte where our air support is needed.

November 5
The cruiser Reno *is torpedoed. She was in our task group. The explosion woke me up.*

November 7
We are being attacked by the so-called Kamikaze or enemy suicide planes. One plane dives into a carrier but only damages her island. Another dives into the Ticonderoga, *a new carrier that has recently joined us only to overshoot her mark, then crashes in the ocean causing a tremendous explosion.*

November 8
Our sister the North Carolina *is back with us again.*

November 10
All night G.Q. Attacked again. No hits scored by the enemy.

November 16
Going back to Ulithi.

November 17
Drop anchor. Gosh, but this heat is unbearable. Just as soon stay out to sea.

November 18
Received Xmas gift from Sis.

November 21
Leave Ulithi for Philippines. Kamikaze -- Divine Winds -- crash into Essex. *Nothing exciting happened this time.*

December 1
Return to Ulithi. Irbin gets transferred. Weigh 148 pounds. Received records from Marie – all in pieces. Tch!

(Irbin was a storekeeper and a very good artist who drew a lot of sketches for our ship's paper.)

December 14
Leave Ulithi for Luzon area. While in port the Wisconsin *joined the fleet - also a number of cruisers including the* Pasadena -- *Wilson (a storekeeper friend) is on it.*

December 18
We are in the center of a typhoon. It plays havoc with this fleet. The roughest sea I have ever been in. We make a 28 degree list, the biggest since this ship went into commission. Three small ships (DE's) capsize losing most of its complements. One carrier loses all its planes. Almost every ship suffers minor damages on its decks.

December 24
Arrive in Ulithi. Midnight Mass. Received letters (packet) from Dot, gifts from Maxie. Provision ship. Wilson pays us a visit. See some good movies.

December 30
Leave port. Alabama *goes to the States – lucky devils.*

1945

January 2
We are heading north. Temperature drops to 75 degrees. Feels cold but like it. The invasion of Luzon is slated for the 5th. We will oper-ate in the China Sea between Formosa and Luzon. That's hot territory all right. But the closer the better. Last month, in one of their raids on Saipan, the Japs hit the Post Office. We had some mail there. Also, one of the tin cans that as lost in the storm had a few bags of mail for us.

January 6
We are between Formosa and Luzon. D day is on the 9th. Mucky weather makes poor results. Our objective is to hit airfields on Formosa and islands around it

January 7
Head south, fuel. Luzon hit by our planes.

January 8
Temperature down to 61 degrees. Cold - perfect weather.

January 9
Our forces invade Luzon. Opposition light -- as yet. We go through the straits and tomorrow we'll be in the China Sea. Will fuel Friday -- west of Manila.

January 10
This morning we were 82 miles south of Formosa and 200 and some odd miles from Hong Kong. Perfect weather.

January 11
Fuel ship from tanker. Tonight we will steam at full speed in a south westerly direction for a strike tomorrow. Appears to be a Jap force or convoy in that area.

January 12
Baie de Camranh -- French Indo China only 40 miles away. Our planes attack shipping in the bay and other ports along the coast.

January 14
Hainan being hit by our planes today.

January 16
Still going south. Hong Kong, Amoy and Swatow are today's objectives.

January 17
While fueling in very rough waters, a coxswain was killed when water broke over the beam and crushed him against a gun mount.

January 19
We cross the straits and return to the Pacific Ocean head north.
Beautiful calm seas. Temperature down to 61. On the 17th while
fueling at sea a coxswain was killed when water broke over the beam
and crushed him against a gun mount.

January 20
Kamikazes attack. We open fire first time this year. Two Jap planes
dive on and crash into the Ticonderoga *air craft carrier.* Langley *hit*
also. One bomb explodes causing slight damage.

January 27
Will enter port.

January 28
Enter port. Transfer for two Chief Storekeepers come in. Oh Maxine,
I must see you soon, so please darling pray that I got transferred.

(Twombly who has been aboard longer than I is expected to be the
one but he asked me if I would take his place. The guy must be nuts to
stay on the ship in the war zone, but we talked to the supply officer
and he approved my transfer. Whoopee. Twombly and I both made
chief at the same time. After passing our exams, we had to take a
typing test which required at least 40 words per minute. Poor Twombly
could hardly type, so after finishing mine, I did his also. What the heck,
this was war time and all they could do was bust me. Nevertheless,
thank you buddy.)

January 29
Gangway son for it is Uncle Sugar for me. Thanks Maxie, your
prayers for me were heard.

January 30
Fleet will pull out tomorrow noon for unknown destination. If we
do not get transportation before then, we will have to make the trip.
Oh, but I hope not.

(They arranged transportation for the group or six or seven of us
leaving on the Independence. *We must get off the ship before noon and*
it is real choppy and there are nets along side for us to climb down to
the boat taking us to the carrier. Threw my sea bag into the boat and
scrambled down yelling goodbye to my shipmates. Fleet pulls out and
the Independence *heads for home.)*

February 1
Aboard the USS Independence. *Maxie, here I come. Fleet pulls out.*
So long pals, especially you from the might "W" – good lucky and
God bless you all.

My Days After Leaving the USS *Washington*

I t sure was nice to be back in the islands. Stayed with my Sister Nani and just enjoyed the local food again. It was the first time I had poi in years and the rest of the Hawaiian food to go with it. Had to report back every day to wait for transportation to San Francisco, where I would be assigned to my new ship.

Within two weeks we got a transport ship and it took ten long days to reach San Francisco. It was the worse trip I ever experienced in my navy career. There must have been two thousand troops aboard and the bunks were at least 10 high or more. No showers available and only two meals a day. Got through eating breakfast and you had to stand in line to have your second meal. The lines were so long you had no other choice and the tables were built high so that you stood up and ate your meal. Sure was glad to get to San Francisco after ten long, long days.

I arrived in San Francisco and went to Treasure Island which lies in the middle of the Oakland bay bridge. Got interviewed and they told me that they would send me to the receiving station nearest to my home. Because I had never been to the east coast, I felt that here was my chance to cheat a little. When in Hawaii I played golf with a friend named Mino who lived in Brooklyn, New York and I remembered his address because he always used to tell me to be sure to say hello to his mom and dad in the event that I arrived in that area before he got home. The next morning my name was paged on the squawk box and I told them I lived at 274 Prospect Ave., Brooklyn, New York. Although I was nervous, it was obvious that they accepted what I had said. Come back in the morning the yeoman told me and we should have your orders ready.

The next morning they informed me that I was eligible to take some leave due to the extensive duties I had just been through so I asked them if I could go to Seattle before going to New York. They told me that they would give me transportation from coast to coast but I had to pay my own way to Seattle, which I agreed.

Two days later, I was on a train headed for Seattle. Dottie was waiting for me at the train station and we spent a wonderful two weeks doing nothing but enjoying each others love. As usual time goes by fast when you are having fun and it had to end.

I got a train heading for New York City. Reported to the receiving station on Flushing Avenue in Brooklyn, right across the street from the Brooklyn Naval Shipyard. After about two weeks, my name was called and I had my orders to report to the Material Redistribution Office right across the street at the Shipyard. I could not believe that I was getting shore duty instead of a new ship as expected. Whoopee!

The office was made up of three officers, a Lieutenant Commander, a Lieutenant and an Ensign, about six or seven Chief Petty Officers and around 24 or 25 women, all of them between the ages of eighteen and the oldest was twenty six. Talk about being in Heaven. Blondes, brunettes, red heads, unbelievable. After all those years at sea and now I have to suffer this happiness.

One weekend I decided do go visit the family of that buddy of mine that lived in Brooklyn. So I headed for 274 Prospect Avenue and met the Minos. They were real surprised to see me and mentioned that their son said I would be in the area. They treated me like a lost son and it was wonderful meeting such nice wonderful people. They are Italians so we had chicken cacciatore for dinner and it was delicious. They offered me a room to sleep in and thanked them for the offer and their hospitality. Had dinner and returned three or four more times to enjoy their company and the good food while I was in New York.

Another Chief and myself found a fifth floor walk-up apartment at 91st and Columbus in upper Manhattan with a bar right on the corner and made ourselves comfortable. During that period food was rationed so we had to make do with what we could connive. Being in uniform and having a few battle stars got you a long way in New York City. You could not have been treated any better in any other city the way they treated you. They showed respect and were very generous with all military personnel. Thank you New York City!

In a short time, I got acquainted with Ann, one of the ladies in the office and we started dating and having dinner together. She lived on 81st and Amsterdam. Although it was only about ten blocks away, in that town each block seems like a mile long so it takes a subway ride to see her. Anyway, time goes by and we just got along and had fun.

One day my Dad writes that Arthur my cousin whose Dad did not want him to get in the Navy was at the Naval Shipyard in Brooklyn. He had joined the navy after the war started and was on a PT boat at the landings on Omaha beach in Europe. What a trip. I called the shipyard left a message and the next day he called me; it was quite a reunion with two local Hawaiian boys in the big city.

Ann had a sister named Francis who worked in the same office we did so we made a dinner date and the four of us went out and there the story begins. A few weeks later they advised us that they were getting married, I could hardy believe it but it happened. They got married at a local Catholic church and the reception was held at the St. Regis Hotel where Ray Kinney, a Hawaiian group, played the Hawaiian Wedding Song. Unbelievable and it was chicken skin time with tears.

In August 1945 the Japanese surrendered after two atomic bombs were dropped on them. I had taken my boss to a meeting at a hotel in Times Square the day the war ended. He told me to take in a movie since they would be having lunch after the meeting. When I got out of the movie, Times Square was so full of people and I found out the war had ended. Met my boss and we were not able to get the car out because of the people; so he told me to have fun there with the rest of the crowd and pick the car up in the morning. That night some girl from New Jersey took me home. Oh what a night.

My Days After the War

I had enough points for a discharge but all storekeepers and yeomen were frozen and ordered to go to the Lido Beach Hotel in Long Island to establish a Separation Center for navy personnel coming home. The first day we had about twenty five people go through and it got more every day so we added more in-house personnel. We processed more than two or three hundred a day as time went on. It was not an easy job. My job was to review one small section of the paper work then put a stamp on it. After a while you just stamped it without even checking if the spelling was correct. It was boring and I was aching to go home. In December they put out a new list of those eligible to leave and my name was on the top of the list. Goodbye Long Island. You were nice but now is the time to say Aloha.

My wish was to see some of the country and I felt the best way to do it was by getting on a bus. I must say that it was quite an experience. I cannot recall the occasion, but there was something big going on in Chicago. So I decided to spend a day or two there. I got off the bus, hailed a cab and asked to be taken to a reasonable hotel. He told me that I had better get back on the bus because it was impossible to get any room with whatever was going on. So back on the bus.

The next stop I decided was Denver. And would you believe, they, too, had some kind of convention -- for farmers around the country to show off their bulls. And there, too, no hotels were available. So off to Salt Lake City. Sunday there and local laws said no-no to booze. We headed to the train station and slept there until we got on the train the next morning.

They put me on a Hospital ship for my return to Hawaii and I was assigned a cabin in the officer's quarters. Big deal all right but it felt a little uncomfortable whenever they asked us what our ranks were. There were three other enlisted men as passengers and we were told to wear civilian clothes; consequently, no one knew what our ranks were. After the second day we felt a little more comfortable and enjoyed the ride.

What a blessing to get back home. I finally made it back to Kauai to visit my Dad and the many relatives and old time buddies. Of course the next thing to do was to find a job. With the millions of military going home it would not be easy.

After about three weeks I returned to Honolulu. The City and County of Honolulu had an ad asking for men to join the police force and I applied. The first thing they did was make me get on a scale and I weighed 149 pounds. The sergeant told me to go home, eat some bananas and come back tomorrow as the minimum weight was 150 pounds. Did that; I ate a few and the next day I was accepted for the next recruit training as I met the correct weight.

I decided to go back to Kauai for a short rest and be prepared to start a new career. As the days went by and meeting with my Dad and Uncle who felt that there were other jobs better then the police force, I changed my mind and decided to get back in the navy. At that time there was a two year enlistment available; so I re-enlisted with the intentions to get out after that period when jobs would probably be easier to find.

They assigned me to the Yards and Docks Supply Depot which was located between Ewa beach and the Naval Ammunition Depot at West Loch, Pearl Harbor. The Depot was the dumping grounds for heavy equipment and all modes of transportation available and in reasonable operating conditions. There were many warehouses on the base and each was stocked with materials coming from overseas facilities that were no longer active. The items included binoculars, cameras, projectors and whatever was required by the military to function.

The fact that the war was over and the majority of military being reserves, a shortage of personnel became a serious problem. The other problem was that there never was an inventory of what was in the warehouses. Consequently, nothing was really missed if it were stolen.

In the meantime, the Commanding Officer assigned Chief Petty Officers to each of the warehouses who had no concept of supply procedures so I will not go into what eventually turned into a court martial for a few Chiefs. It was sad to see some of your friends get busted but they were old enough to know that it was wrong to take things that did not belong to them.

As for myself, I too got in trouble for signing property passes for the trucks that removed the items that we eventually auctioned off to contractors. The chief in charge would give me the list of items being removed and I signed the passes for the command only to find out later that there was more material on the trucks then what showed on the paper work. Fortunately, the Commanding Officer decided that it was not my fault and that was one big relief.

Raising a Family

While working there I met the cutest local Japanese girl working as a waitress in a club and made frequent visits. Her name was Ruth and she thought I was not a local boy until we started dating. It was not long before I felt that we should get married. After the normal period of time we had our first child and named him after myself. His middle name being Kameeiamoku, we shortened it and for some reason or other we always called him Kammy.

Then came my second son Joseph Mahoe whom we call Jay; third was Ronald when we were living in Japan and I was stationed at the Naval Supply Depot in Yokosuka and assigned to the ComServRonThree staff. The majority of the staff were on a ship in the harbor.

Kammy and Jay attended schools wherever we were stationed – and there were many (16 in all). In Japan, they attended a Christian Brothers School (St. Joseph's College) and were the only U.S. citizens; it was an indoctrination of its own. The Brothers or teachers were very strict, each wielding a bamboo stick which they were not hesitant to use. They required the Japanese students to speak English from the third grade on. My sons reported after the first day that if the students spoke Japanese, a book would fly through the room, normally hitting the student. Students learned English fast.

As time passed (and too fast I would tell myself), the boys grew up. Kammy was an honors student throughout all his school years and had numerous scholarship offers. He chose the University of San Francisco and finished the ROTC program. He was named a Distinguished Military Graduate and received a Regular Army Commission along with his BA degree in Sociology.

He served with the 173d Airborne Brigade for nearly 2 years in Vietnam in various combat positions with the Field Artillery and Infantry. He was awarded the Purple Heart twice and decorated for heroism a number of times, which he never talks about. Kammy never boasted of what he did in Vietnam. He's just that sort of guy.

He retired from the US Army with 20 years of service as an Airborne Ranger, Jumpmaster, Pathfinder and Aviator. After 10 years on active duty, he resigned his Regular Army commission to take a position with GTE Hawaiian Tel and joined the Army Reserve. After 10 years with them in various public relations and marketing positions, he formed his own management consulting firm with clients in Hawaii, the Pacific Region and Asia – including some Native American Tribes and other native indigenous groups in the Pacific Basin.

Another war veteran in our family, my second son Jay joined the Navy in 1969 and served in Vietnam as a radioman aboard the USS *Flint*. In 1979 he re-enlisted in the California Army National Guard. He graduated from the California Military Academy and was commissioned in 1980 as a Second Lieutenant in the Military Police. His unit was activated for the Persian Gulf War, and there he commanded a unit responsible for the security of a POW camp on the outskirts of Kuwait. In his civilian life, he also finished a 30-year career in the police force with Redwood City, California. Like his older brother, he retired as an Army major. Still continuing in a lifetime career of serving and protecting, he works for Home Land Security at the Oakland airport.

My third son Ron graduated from San Francisco State University with a degree in Communications. He has enjoyed a very successful and varied career in the broadcasting industry. From being a program director at various radio stations, to editor of R&R magazine (a national trade magazine for radio stations), to PR specialist at XM Sirius Radio, to now an analyst for Nielsen in Maryland – the folks that provide all that survey information businesses and politicians seek for decision-making.

In 1960, sometime while stationed at the Naval Ammunition Depot in Lualualei, Oahu, Ruth and I split. We had differences and she eventually married a guy named Pete, who was a navy friend of mine. It sure is funny how some things just work out for the best – for all concerned.

On my last tour of duty in the Navy, I was assigned to the Pacific Nuclear Weapons Training Facility at the Naval Air Station across the bay from San Diego, California. They put me with the Inspection Department and this entailed a lot of traveling. We inspected any Navy or Marine facility having the Nuclear Weapons Capability which included all the West Coast of the U.S. and all activities in the Pacific. Much of the travel was done commercial and during those days most of it was on United Air Lines. So at least we traveled in somewhat comfortable means which meant a lot with the amount of travel we did. I accumulated more than two hundred thousand miles during my three year tour of duty there. It did get tiresome especially when going from one climate to another where you needed warmer clothes and had to pack extra.

On returning to Hawaii after my retirement in 1964, there was a twelve month payment of fifty dollars a week to all military personnel who qualified. To receive this payment, one was required to show proof that they applied for a position with any type of company. After one month of not accepting positions, mostly because of the hours, I decided to look for something more suitable to my Navy experience. I applied for a position at the Naval Supply Center as a Fork Lift Operator, knowing that once I got in, there would be room for advancement. It did not take long before one of the foreman in the group was sick, and because of my background, I was asked to fill in temporarily. It lasted almost eight months until I applied for a Warehouse Foreman position that was open at the General Services Administration. I was interviewed by the Customer Supply Officer Jack Bauer and the Manager of the Depot Bill Akiona, and then offered the position. When Bill retired, I was offered his position. The GSA Depot was eventually closed and we downsized to a Self Service Store. I then became the Manager of the store and eventually the name was changed to the Customer Supply

Center. Together with my one year at the Naval Supply Center, I retired with thirty years of service, this time as a civilian with the Federal Government on August 1, 1994.

It was on one of my trips to Honolulu during my last tour in the Navy that I met my second wife. I went to visit my sister Nani and there I met Louise Brown. My sister was at work that day so I decided to make some dinner for them that night, some kind of chili and beans without the chili. When Louise came home with my sister, she was invited to dinner and thanked me for being a good cook.

That night my sister asked me if I wanted to go to the Chiefs club in Pearl Harbor to a dance and I agreed since Louise was going with her. All this time I was in civilian clothing. On the way to the club, Louise asked my sister if they would let me in. When we got to the club, they did let me in because I had to show my ID. It was then that Louise found out I was in the navy.

On my next trip to Honolulu which was about a month later, I asked Louise out for dinner and on the following trip, about two months later, we got married.

Louise already had four children from a previous marriage -- Jimmy, Mary, Stella and Fred. Now with four of hers, three of mine (from my first marriage) plus two of ours it adds up to nine in the family. And we are still one happy family. It is mine, hers and ours. Nice, huh!

Jimmy now lives in Granite Falls, Washington and has thirty-some acres of space for his business. He sells rocks to folks in Seattle mostly that want rock gardens, plus he has trucks to support whatever a customer requires. He also has equipment to grade roads. Jimmy is innovative, a very go-go guy and never afraid of work.

Mary was quite a girl in her younger days. She was active in a Junior

Achievement group and always had the best grades. She attended the University of Hawaii, got married to Tony, and had a boy named Tony. Her son is doing very well today and is a honcho in a new restaurant in Kona on the Big Island. He went to college in Boulder Colorado; worked in San Jose, California for a while but decided there was no place like paradise, so he returned home to Hawaii.

After graduation, finding a teachers position in Hawaii was not easy, so Mary accepted a job in California and taught there for a few years. The there was an opening for an English school in Germany and she took little Tony with her and they stayed there for a couple of years. In the meantime, Sister and her husband Tony separated and divorced.

From Germany, Mary (whom we always called Sister) returned to Hawaii and worked for the Kamehameha schools for about two years; then for the last twenty plus years at Punahou School, one of the most prestigious schools in the Islands.

Sister is now married to Morrie Pinker the best New Zealander one will ever get to know. He is the most congenial person to have around. We all appreciate him very much. He is a jewel of all jewels. He is a master carpenter and built their house in the Holualoa district of Kona on the Big Island; and it is a palace.

Stella lives in San Diego, California and is a salesperson for eye glass frames. Her territory includes Las Vegas, the Hawaiian islands and naturally the San Diego vicinity. She brought one of her cars to use in Hawaii and has logged more than four hundred thousand miles. I thought my Ford with eighty thousand miles was a lot until she told me how much she traveled in hers. She is in Hawaii every six weeks so we see her often. At least all the time we pick her up and take her back to the airport. But that is what Grandpas do for a living.

Fred, the youngest of the Brown bunch, lives in Greeley, Colorado and is the luckiest one. He won a six million dollar lottery; and was smart enough to take in increments over a twenty year period. He went to college in Greeley, married a girl name Barbara and have two wonderful children named Andrew and Allison.

I have visited them, in the summer time of course (do not like snowy weather) and enjoyed the visit. Fred worked at a Ford Company dealership and broke all records in sales. The company was sold and Fred moved on and is now in a teaching position and am glad for him. One needs to keep busy, no matter how much money you have.

I now live in Kailua on the windward side of the island in a community called Maunawili. It is in a secluded area surrounded by the Koolau mountains. I must thank my wife Louise who found the place through a lady friend of hers who was a realtor. This is the longest period that I have lived in the same house since I was born.

Louise and I had two children and both were born at the Tripler Army Medical Center here in Honolulu. Our son Kalani was born when we were living at Lunaapono Place in lower Maunawili, and our beautiful daughter Aulani arrived two years later. When Kalani was old enough, he started delivering the evening newspaper with about a hundred fifty subscribers that kept him very busy every afternoon. On Sunday mornings, either Mom or Dad gave him a hand assembling the paper as it arrived around 5 a.m. and off he went. When he got his driver's license at fifteen years old, he used our Datsun pickup and that made it easier.

He attended junior college for two years and found his niche in the entertainment business. Today he works for the largest stage and lighting company in Honolulu and is doing very well. He started with six moving lights and stored them in our garage; today he has ten times that many and the company he works for has two large warehouses where he can store them.

Aulani my youngest daughter lives with me and her family; she is now also my care giver. She is a clone of my wife, a gourmet cook, has a great sense of humor, and always keeps her cool no matter the situation. In her younger days we did a lot of traveling as a family which we always enjoyed, especially the various Historical Parks.

When she was old enough, she and a girl friend went to Dutch Harbor where their boy friends were deck hands on a commercial fishing boat. While there, she worked at the only restaurant in town and learned how to cook. After about a year she returned home.

She has three boys: Austin who just graduated from Kailua High School (June 2011) Dustin just turning six and going into first grade; and Keahi just two and in pre-school and boss of the house. I do a lot of cartoon watching whenever my daughter has chores and I do some baby sitting which I enjoy. It is payback time for all my daughter does for me.

To keep myself active, I volunteer at the Arizona Memorial Visitor Center; the name was changed to Pacific Historic Parks recently. There were many ships and other military activities that were damaged on December 7, 1941. Fairness to all is one of the reasons for the name change.

There are five Pearl Harbor survivors that volunteer here three times a week. We sit at a table and autograph a biography of ourselves and items purchased at the Museum book store. We may sign more than two hundred each day we volunteer. It is interesting to meet people from many foreign countries and every state in the Union.

On many of the pages, my diary was written with a pencil and it was getting hard to read. So at the prompting of my eldest son Kammy, I decided that it was time to put this into print so that my children and grandchildren are able to know and understand what I did in my navy career.

In closing, I want to remind people that we should honor the memories of my generation so that we can pass to future generations the stories of what those brave, heroic men and women of World War II did to preserve our freedom. Freedom is not free.

Alfred Benjamin Kameeiamoku Rodrigues, SKC, USN (Ret.),
June 30, 2011

Alfred and his wife Louise

Alfred with fellow Pearl Harbor Survivor Bob Kinzler, another volunteer at the Pearl Harbor Visitor Center.

Facts about USS *Washington* (BB-56)

Second of two battleships in the North Carolina *class*
Keel laid down on 14 June 1938
Launched on 1 June 1940
Commissioned on 15 May 1941
Decommissioned 27 June 1947
Displacement of 35,000 tons
Length of 729 feet
Beam of 108 feet
Draft of 38 feet
Speed of 27 knots
Crew 108 officers, 1,772 men
Armament 9 x 16 inch guns, 20 x 5 inch guns,
    16 x 1 inch machine guns
Aircraft carried 3 x SOC Seagull
Honors and Awards 13 Battle Stars

USS *Washington* has the distinction being the the only American battleship to sink an enemy battleship (Japanese *Kirishima*) during World War II in a one-on-one surface engagement. She suffered no losses to hostile action during the entire course of the war.

In August she was deployed to the Pacific for action against Imperial Japan, where she became the flagship of Rear Admiral Willis Augustus Lee. Two months after her arrival at Tonga in September 1942, *Washington* was tasked with intercepting a Japanese naval task force near Guadalcanal along with *South Dakota* and four destroyers. In the ensuing battle, *South Dakota* was severely damaged, but *Washington* sustained almost no damage while her guns sank the battleship *Kirishima* and the destroyer *Ayanami*. *Washington* operated as an escort for aircraft carrier task forces for most of 1943, and together with five other battleships bombarded Nauru in December. Around dawn on 1 February 1944, *Washington* rammed the battleship *Indiana* and incurred several fatalities when the latter was maneuvering across the formation to refuel destroyers. With around 60 feet of her bow heavily damaged, *Washington* was forced to retire. The Pearl Harbor shipyards fitted the battleship with a temporary bow; a full restoration had to wait until the ship could dock in the Puget Sound Navy Yard.

Washington arrived back in the Pacific war zone in mid-1944. She took part in bombarding Saipan and Tinian before joining the Battle of the Philippine Sea. For the rest of the war, *Washington* alternated between shore bombardment and carrier escort, including direct support in the battles of Iwo Jiwa and Okinawa. In July 1945, the battleship headed for the Puget Sound Navy Yard for a badly needed overhaul. She did not emerge until October, after the end of the war. On November 2, she was assigned to Operation Magic Carpet, the withdrawal of American military personnel from overseas deployments

Glossary

- *Bogey – airplane sighting*
- *Cans – tin cans, destroyers*
- *Dope -- news*
- *Focsle – forward part of a ship*
- *G.Q. – General Quarters*
- *Gunnorf – term used for gunnery practice on the Hawaii Island of Kahoolawe*
- *Helen – nickname for the Japanese Nakajima KI-49 bomber*
- *Pollywog – someone who is about to cross the International Date Line for the first time*
- *Scuttlebutt – rumor*
- *SK 1C – rank of Storekeeper First Class*
- *S.P. – Shore Patrol*
- *Mele Kalikimaka – Hawaiian for Merry Christmas*